Essex*Works.*

For a better quality of life

PRE

D0588223

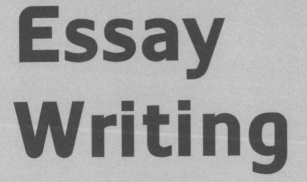

Essay
Writing

The *Student Essentials* series

Student Essentials: Critical Thinking
Student Essentials: Dissertation
Student Essentials: Essay Writing
Student Essentials: Revision and Exam Strategies
Student Essentials: Study Skills

STUDENT ESSENTIALS

Essay Writing

Sophie Fuggle

trotman t

Student Essentials: *Essay Writing*

This first edition published in 2011 by Trotman Publishing, a division of Crimson Publishing Ltd, Westminster House, Kew Road, Richmond, Surrey TW9 2ND

© Trotman Publishing 2011

Author Sophie Fuggle

Designed by Andy Prior

British Library Cataloguing in Publication Data
A catalogue record for this book is available from the British Library

ISBN 978 1 84455 273 3

Typeset by IDSUK (Data Connection) Ltd

Printed and bound in the UK by Ashford Colour Press, Gosport, Hants

Contents

Introduction: Staring at a blank page   1

Part 1: Planning your essay (and your time)   3

A few words on time management   5
Work backwards   5
Some sample timetables   6

CHAPTER 1
The question   9
Choosing the question   9
Understanding the question: different formats   11
Tips for top scores   14
Checklist   15

CHAPTER 2
Researching the topic   16
Selecting your sources   16
Using your sources   17
Focusing your secondary reading   18
Recording sources   19
Accessing texts   19

Sources to avoid   21
Tips for top scores   23
Checklist   23

CHAPTER 3
Organising your ideas   **24**
Making a plan   24
Structuring your argument   25
Different essay models   29
Tips for top scores   33
Checklist   33

Part 2: Writing your essay   **35**

CHAPTER 4
Beginnings and endings   **37**
Different approaches to writing your introduction   37
Powerful conclusions   43
Tips for top scores   46
Checklist   47

CHAPTER 5
Making your point   **48**
Signposting your argument   48
Avoiding the strawmen   50
Selecting quotations and examples   51
Tips for top scores   54
Checklist   55

CHAPTER 6
Writing with style   **56**
Developing a strong narrative   56
Good and bad writing   58
Tips for top scores   65
Checklist   66

Part 3: Essay presentation 67

CHAPTER 7
References and bibliography 69
How to use footnotes and endnotes 69
Author–date referencing 70
Style guides: a quick guide 71
Abbreviated references 73
Other material included in footnotes and endnotes 74
Setting out your bibliography 75
Tips for top scores 78
Checklist 79

CHAPTER 8
Formatting your work 80
Using data, graphs and images 80
General essay presentation 82
Spelling and grammar 87
Layout and spacing 88
Tips for top scores 88
Checklist 89

CHAPTER 9
Developing your technique 90
Effective proofreading 90
Learning from the process 91
Learning from feedback 92
Improving your writing style over the long term 93
Tips for top scores 94
Checklist 95

Essay writing Q & A 96

Glossary 99

Introduction: Staring at a blank page

When faced with an essay, do you end up staring at a blank piece of paper or computer screen for hours, if not days? Does your essay end up being written in a state of panic the night before the deadline? Do you end up with pages and pages of incoherent notes which you struggle to organise? If you're reading this, the chances are that one or more of the above situations applies to you, or perhaps you just want to work on improving your essay writing technique. *Student Essentials: Essay Writing* is aimed at taking the pain out of essay writing, while also providing you with a step-by-step guide to improving your technique.

Each chapter will cover a specific aspect of essay writing, from choosing which question to answer, to understanding examiners' feedback. Although each chapter builds upon the previous one, you can choose whether to read the book from cover to cover or simply dip into it for helpful tips. A glossary is also provided to clarify common technical terms which might be used in relation to essay writing either in the book itself or by your lecturers and examiners.

Students who have already developed good essay technique will also benefit from our *Tips for top scores*, which suggest ways you can enhance your style and structure even further to ensure maximum grades.

Thinking of an essay as something to 'get through' or 'survive' is one of the biggest hurdles to developing good technique. This is because it fails to take into account the fact that the essay will be read by someone else. If you perceive essay writing as a form of torture, there is a strong chance you will pass on this suffering to the person reading it. Start thinking about the essay not as something you **have to write** but as something your examiner **has to read**. This will keep you focused throughout the essay writing process on **why** your essay should be interesting, original and perhaps even fun to read. The chapters which follow will show you **how** to achieve this.

PART 1

Planning your essay (and your time)

Careful planning makes essay writing a whole lot easier and helps prevent last-minute disasters. The first three chapters are dedicated to the planning process. Specific focus will be given to managing your time efficiently, choosing which question to tackle and how to set about researching your topic. We will then look at various ways of organising and structuring your essay to ensure that the writing process goes as smoothly as possible.

A few words on time management

Let's be realistic: no matter how good our intentions are, devising a timetable of work and sticking faithfully to it is near impossible. Time set aside to work on an essay is frequently conceded to searching for non-existent library books or dealing with broken laptops.

Giving yourself enough time to plan, write and revise your essay might seem a luxury given other deadlines and commitments. However, not allowing yourself enough time to plan, write and revise your essay will prevent you getting the best possible mark. Formulating a timetable of work which takes into account other obligations and allows room for potential problems will ensure that you dedicate enough time to your essay and perhaps even avoid having to pull an all-nighter.

Work backwards

Take a blank piece of paper. Write the deadline date at the top and the current date at the bottom. Work out how many days, weeks or even months there are between those two dates. Divide the time into three. The first third should be dedicated to thinking about the question and compiling a reading list, the second third should be spent reading and planning, and the final third should be reserved for writing and revising your essay. Depending on the essay topic you have chosen and your own working rhythm, you may want to adjust the length of each third, giving more time to one stage than the others. For example, the reading and planning you need to undertake might require a larger portion of time than writing up your essay.

Be honest with yourself. Are you really going to stay in and read *War and Peace* on a Saturday night? Is it realistic to limit your writing-up time to a single afternoon? Whenever possible give yourself break periods between and during each stage.

Some sample timetables

One-week deadline

- Day 1 – Select essay topic/question. Brainstorm preliminary ideas.
- Day 2 – Go over existing notes. Carry out any secondary reading (given the short deadline, this should be limited to short articles and chapters, not entire volumes).
- Day 3 – Break.
- Day 4 – Write your plan. Sleep on it.
- Day 5 – Write essay.
- Day 6 – Break. Check references.
- Day 7 – Reread essay. Correct/revise as necessary.

Three-week deadline

- Week 1 – Choose essay topic. Preliminary brainstorming. Compile reading list.
- Weekend 1 – Focus on reading.
- Week 2 – Complete reading. Write your plan.
- Weekend 2 – Break.

- Week 3 – Write your essay. Leave it for a couple of days.
- Weekend 3 – Reread essay and revise. Check references.

Two-month deadline

Month 1
- Week 1 – Preliminary brainstorming. Discuss with tutor/lecturer. Compile initial reading list.
- Week 2 – Initial reading. Begin to identify additional reading.
- Weeks 3–4 – Continue reading. Write a first draft of plan.

Month 2
- Week 5 – Break. Continue with reading if necessary.
- Week 6 – Finalise reading list. Complete any supplementary reading.
- Week 7 – Revise essay plan.
- Week 8 – Write essay. Revise and check references.

Having a plan B

Your timetable should aim to maximise the time available to research and write your essay. However, it should also provide you with enough flexibility that in the event of illness or other unforeseen circumstances, you can still meet the deadline without unnecessary stress. University regulations for assessed work tend to be quite rigid, so don't assume that your circumstances will grant you an extension. Work on finishing your essay in time while you are waiting for official confirmation on this from your department.

The perils of printing

If you don't own a printer, give yourself enough time to print out your essay at your university library or IT centre. Make sure your essay is saved in a format that can be read by your university computers. Familiarise yourself with alternative print options, such as copy shops, in case of problems with university printing. Multiple coursework deadlines often fall on the same day, so avoid the queues by printing your essay the day before. If you have your own printer, make sure you have enough ink and paper a few days before the essay is due.

1 The question

Answer the question. Answer the question. Answer the question. This is possibly the most important piece of advice anyone can give you and you should repeat it as a mantra throughout the essay writing process. While this might seem obvious, an alarming number of students either misread the question or take it as an invitation to write about anything vaguely related to the topic at hand. To avoid this, make sure you fully understand what is being asked of you before you start researching and writing your essay.

Choosing the question

Faced with a list of essay questions, it is important that you select a question which enables you to show in-depth knowledge of the subject you are dealing with and which allows you to focus your discussion on the specific problems posed by the essay question. Remember that you have studied a particular area of knowledge and the essay you write must demonstrate how successfully you have got to grips with the topics covered in the course. Here are some tips.

- Avoid the temptation to pick the first question which jumps out at you. Consider all questions carefully before making your decision. Sometimes the more difficult questions force you to think much harder about the subject and so result in a more tightly argued essay. But don't just pick a question that sounds difficult because you think it will impress your lecturer.

- Don't be deceived by the apparent simplicity of a question. A seemingly open-ended question can be very seductive as it appears to invite you to write about any and every aspect of the topic or set of topics you have been studying. An open-ended question might ask you to explain a very broad topic or concept (e.g. 'What is time?') with reference to texts and examples of your choice. You need to remember, though, that while the scope of the question might be broad, your essay needs to demonstrate close reading and solid evidence rather than sweeping statements and generalisations.
- Don't dismiss a question because it sounds too specific and, by implication, restrictive. The narrow scope of a question may turn out to be useful in helping you to focus your reading and give you pointers as to how to organise your argument. There will always be room for you to develop your argument beyond the question itself.

When choosing a question, be realistic about the level of work involved as well as your own abilities.

To help you choose a topic which you feel confident dealing with, ask yourself the following questions.

- Which of the topics covered in the module did you find most interesting?
- Which topic offers the most potential for debate?
- How well have you understood the primary material?
- Did you experience any difficulties with the set reading for particular topics? Might this pose a problem for certain questions?
- Is a good selection of secondary reading material available?

Pre-empting possible problems and difficulties early on prevents you wasting time on a particular essay topic only to have to change it later.

Understanding the question: different formats

Identify the format of the question and use this to decipher what the question is really asking. Essay questions often take the form of statements designed to encourage debate. They may also include a key quotation intended to inspire your own engagement with a particular concept, text or period. Make sure you are clear about both the phrasing of the question and all the terms used.

Often the key to how you should set about formatting your answer is provided by the question itself. Does it want you to argue for and against a particular viewpoint, concept or practice? Are there multiple components which you need to consider in turn? Use the format of the question to help you understand what format your answer should take.

Here are some examples of different question formats:

> ❝ Why was Paris often described as the 'capital of modernity'? Is this view justified? ❞

There are two parts to the question: you need to answer both.

> ❝ The poet must become more and more comprehensive, more allusive, more indirect, in order to force, to dislocate if necessary, language into

QUICK TIP

If a quotation is used, look it up so that you fully understand the context, i.e. why it was written and what it means.

his meaning.' Discuss Eliot's statement with reference to two or more poets studied. **"**

This question is based on a quotation which you should use to direct your answer.

" *Review the achievements and limitations to date of attempts to recover and interpret ancient human DNA, and discuss the future prospects of research in this field.* **"**

The structure of the essay is provided by the question.

Unpacking the question

To ensure that you fully understand a question, you can break it down into smaller parts. Using one of the above sample questions, here is a quick guide to unpacking an essay question.

Divide the question into manageable parts according to how many clauses or sentences it has.

1. Why was Paris often described as the 'capital of modernity'?

2. Is this view justified?

Then circle all the words you think are important – see Figure 1 on page 13.

Breaking down the question shouldn't take more than 5–10 minutes and will give you a realistic idea of what will be involved in producing the essay. It will also help you avoid misreading the question before you start planning the essay.

Figure 1: Breaking down the question

Why – the 'question' word should define how you construct your answer. While you also need to establish 'who' described Paris as the 'capital of modernity', 'how' they did this and in 'what' context they made this statement – it is the 'why' that should constitute the focus of your discussion.

'often described' – suggests you need to discuss more than one instance in which Paris has been described as the 'capital of modernity'.

1. Why was Paris often described as the 'capital of modernity'?

Paris – this is the primary object of your discussion. However, although it is clear that you should talk about Paris, this is a very broad topic so you will have to decide which aspects to concentrate on, e.g. architecture, artists, etc.

'capital of modernity' – this indicates the texts or examples you should concentrate on (those where Paris is described or presented in these terms), the period of Parisian history you should focus on (modernity is usually used to describe the 19th and early 20th centuries) and the terms you will need to define. Does 'capital of modernity' suggest that Paris defined itself as a capital city during the 19th century or does it mean that Paris represented **the** city of modernity?

2. Is this view justified?

Is this view justified? – here you have the opportunity to develop your own argument. Do you agree or disagree with the statement that 'Paris represents the capital of modernity'?

Remember, you will need to provide evidence to back up your argument. In this case, you could either compare Paris to other cities during the same period, such as New York or London, or look at the status and identity of Paris during other historical periods.

Designing your own question

Occasionally (though this is more often true of postgraduate essays) your tutor/lecturer will leave it to you to come up with a suitable essay question. This can be quite tricky so it is probably safer to stick with the prescribed list of essay questions. If you are expected to decide upon a title of your choice, always make sure you talk it through with your lecturer or tutor in order to identify any potential problems.

Tips for top scores

■ Make sure the question you pick gives you room to include your own perspective and show evidence of original further reading rather than just rehearsing well-known ideas and arguments.

■ Impress your examiner by identifying the limitations of the question and suggesting ways in which you might broaden its scope to incorporate other arguments.

✓ Dos	✗ Don'ts
✓ Consider each potential question carefully.	✗ Be tempted by 'easy' sounding questions.
✓ Ask for help if you are unsure about the phrasing and/or terminology employed in a question.	✗ Assume you can gloss over a part of a question you don't understand.
✓ Choose a question/ essay topic which you find challenging.	✗ Choose a question which requires an unrealistic amount of reading and research.
	✗ Start researching your essay before deciding on a question.
	✗ Keep changing your essay question or title.

2 Researching the topic

Research is something of a paradox in that you are expected to have a fairly clear idea of what you are looking for before you set out to find it. Having decided which essay question you would like to answer, it is worth having a well-defined list of questions or points in mind when choosing the sources you want to look at. Even if the thrust of your essay and the specific points you end up including shift as a result of closer examination of primary sources and the discovery of exciting secondary literature on the subject, if you don't limit the scope of your research from the outset you will end up with an endless reading list, pages and pages of notes and an essay that refuses to be written.

Selecting your sources

When researching your essay, it is important to define clearly the sources of information which will constitute both the object of your discussion and provide relevant evidence to support the arguments you want to make. It is useful to distinguish between primary and secondary sources.

- **Primary sources** are authentic data, for instance research reports in sciences and social sciences; contemporary accounts of events, such as diaries and speeches in humanities, or novels, paintings, etc. in the arts.

■ **Secondary sources** interpret, analyse and draw conclusions from primary sources. They include textbooks, journal articles and book-length arguments.

Much of what you read, in argument terms, is likely to be a secondary source; interpretations of primary research and therefore contested knowledge. Certain disciplines, such as sciences, history and law, use a lot of primary sources in addition to secondary sources. Don't forget to evaluate primary sources just as critically as secondary sources for accuracy and credibility.

Using your sources

Some essay questions provide a clear definition of the primary sources you need to use. For example, the question might state that you need to refer to a specific text or texts:

> **“** *How does Dickens criticise the Victorian class system in* Hard Times?**”**

It might specify that you need to discuss two or three texts, theories or examples from a predefined list:

> **“** *What is happiness? Discuss with reference to AT LEAST TWO philosophers studied during the course.* **”**

In these cases, **do not** deviate from the instructions as you risk being marked down for not answering the question fully.

Using a single primary source

Where you are given more freedom to define the sources for examination, it is essential to think carefully about the number of sources you want to look at. Looking at a single source gives you the opportunity to carry out a close and sustained examination, but you may need to draw extensively on secondary sources to back up your argument. Ask yourself how confident you feel focusing on just one core text. You will need to ensure that you choose a source which you have a lot to say about with specific reference to the essay question.

Using multiple primary sources

Using two or three primary sources as your focus provides the opportunity to compare and contrast different approaches, styles or narratives in your discussion. As a general rule, it is worth avoiding using more than three or four primary sources – the more objects you have to discuss the less time you have to analyse each one, which can result in a lack of sustained argument and superficial conclusions.

Focusing your secondary reading

Secondary sources should help you clarify your own ideas and provide useful criticism of the primary sources. However, you should never rely on secondary sources to write your essay for you or substitute the commentary of others for your own analysis. Therefore, secondary literature which simply paraphrases your primary sources or tells you what you already know should be referred to sparingly. Try to choose texts which don't simply explain difficult concepts or ideas but which actively critique or develop these ideas in interesting ways.

The art of culling

Be critical. Good research is not only about deciding what to include but also what to exclude. Skim-read potential sources to discern whether they:

- are relevant
- provide original ideas
- are well argued.

Always ask yourself whether quoting or referring to the source will actually enhance your own discussion.

Recording sources

Be sure to keep a clear record of all the sources you read. Write or type out useful quotations accurately. Note down all the relevant bibliographic details for **all** of the texts you look at, including the specific page references of quotations. This will save an enormous amount of time when you come to compile your bibliography (see Chapter 7) and prevent frustrating trips to the library in search of that elusive page number. Keeping a good record of the reading you have done will help you avoid accidentally passing off ideas you have read as your own.

QUICK TIP

Avoid the temptation to 'binge-read' – don't waste valuable time reading every single book and article ever written on your topic. You will only end up confused, overwhelmed and unfocused. Trying to cite an enormous list of secondary sources just to prove you have read them will detract from the argument you are making. It is far better to cite from a few well-chosen references.

Accessing texts
Course and module reading lists

Your first port of call should be the reading lists provided by the course convenor for the module you are studying. This should include key texts that you **must** read as well as criticism and commentaries that the course convenor considers most useful. The texts listed are usually available in the university library or online. Don't make unnecessary work for yourself by trying to build a reading list from scratch. Start with the suggested (sometimes referred to as 'indicative') reading and work from there.

Visit the library

Your choice of reading is often dependent on the texts available in your university library. To ensure you get the best possible range of material to choose from, try to start your research well in advance of the essay deadlines. Ask your tutor or lecturer which texts on the reading list they recommend and if there are any worth buying. If there is a shortage of key texts in the library, ask the course convenor to have these put on short loan so they become available sooner.

Online sources

Most universities also have access to online journals and databases through Athens (an online portal which allows universities to subscribe to a number of online resources). Individual login details are provided to all students. Find out yours and do some preliminary keyword searches to see what articles are available to download. Most likely you will find a variety of different texts related to your essay topic. Start with the most recent, as they will most likely incorporate earlier scholarship, and then work backwards.

Dictionaries, encyclopaedias

These are useful when studying the etymology and evolution of a particular term or idea, **but** simply quoting a dictionary definition will add little to your discussion. Focus instead on defining what the terms **you** are using mean in the context of **your** essay, **not** according to whoever wrote the entry for the *OED*.

Sources to avoid

Not all sources are born equal. When looking for sources to enhance your own argument and discussion it is important to distinguish between opinion, idle speculation and sustained critical engagement from relevant authorities. You wouldn't quote a random man you met in the pub, so why quote random sources of information found on the internet? While this might sound a little dry, your secondary sources should comprise academic monographs, commentaries, textbooks, essays and articles in peer-reviewed journals and edited essay collections.

QUICK TIP

Google books offers you the chance to preview a wide range of academic texts, enabling you to decide whether there is enough relevant material to make a text worth purchasing or hunting down in the library.

What is peer-review?

If an article is published in a peer-reviewed journal or collection of essays it means it has undergone a rigorous editorial process. For it to be accepted for publication, an article will have been blind (anonymously) reviewed by three academics specialising in the subject. Only if the article meets the approval of all of the reviewers will it be published and, even then, the author may be expected to make a number of revisions.

The peer-review process provides you with a certain guarantee that the information presented is both accurate and has stood up to serious criticism and analysis from qualified specialists. You can determine whether a journal is peer-reviewed by visiting its home page (all serious journals should have one, even if they are print journals).

The internet

The internet might seem like a mine of useful information, but it is also a rubbish dump of inaccuracy and uncritical reflection. While forums, blogs and sites like Wikipedia might provide a starting point, you should be highly critical of the information presented in them. Unless the internet forms the object of your study, avoid quoting from unreliable online sources. Again, stick to respected journals, whether online or in print.

QUICK TIP

Never ever use a site that provides pre-written essays, whether these are free or charge a fee. Similarly, do not pay someone else to produce an essay for you. **This is plagiarism** and you risk being kicked off your course if you are caught doing this.

Tips for top scores

- Commentaries and short introductions are useful for ensuring that you have grasped difficult concepts. However, to get top marks it is worth trying to engage with more critical secondary literature. This means articles and longer texts which provide a serious challenge to the concepts or argument you are writing about, or texts offering ways in which these concepts can be developed further using specific examples and case studies.

- Aim to develop your reading beyond the prescribed reading list.

✓ Dos	✗ Don'ts
✓ Limit your primary sources	✗ Try to read everything ever written on a subject.
✓ Focus your secondary reading in relation to the essay question.	✗ Use personal opinion and internet sources uncritically.
✓ Use a range of authoritative sources.	✗ Limit your secondary reading to basic introductions and commentaries.
✓ Make extensive and clearly referenced notes on all the sources you have read.	✗ Pass off someone else's work as your own.

3 Organising your ideas

The key to a good essay is not just what you say but how you say it. Before you start writing your essay it is essential to have a firm idea of how the points you want to make will fit together to form a coherent argument. The more effort you put into planning the structure of your essay, the easier it will be to write it.

Making a plan

Writing a plan seems easy. Putting a series of unrelated points into a list might give the appearance of a well-organised linear argument, but when it comes to writing your essay the logical progression will fall to pieces if you haven't thought seriously about how each point proceeds from the previous one. Similarly, your points might relate too well to every other point in the essay, making it difficult to organise them into a coherent order. In this instance you need to think carefully about how to impose a linear structure on a map or diagram of interrelated ideas without repeating yourself or jumping back and forth between different aspects of your argument.

Mind-mapping

It can be useful to begin your planning with a mind-map. This is a rough diagram in which you explore all the possible connections between the various and disparate ideas you might discuss in an essay or other written project. It can also help you make important decisions about what is extraneous or doesn't fit the main body of your essay. It will also show you the areas of your discussion which need developing. If every point you want to make relates to every other point, perhaps the connections you are making are oversimplified and need further development.

Figure 2, overleaf, is an example of a preliminary mind-map for the following essay question:

> **"** *Are the media reflective or instigative of social and cultural change?* **"**

Having written out a mind-map, you might want to put it aside overnight, or at least for a couple of hours, depending on how much time you have. By returning to it with fresh eyes you will be able to spot the weak links in the connections you have drawn and will begin to develop a clearer idea of the shape the final essay will take.

Structuring your argument

While the mind-map can help identify the major areas of discussion and their relationship to one another, there comes a point where you need to abandon the diagram with its multi-directional arrows and circles and focus on the linear structure of your essay.

When writing a linear plan, be sure to include as much detail as possible. Be clear about exactly how you will use examples rather than simply listing them.

Ask yourself the following questions to help construct your linear argument.

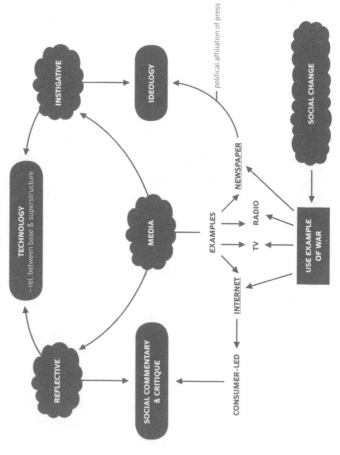

Figure 2: Mind-map for the essay question: *Are the media reflective or instigative of social and culture change?*

- Will it work more effectively to organise my analysis by example (discussing each primary source in turn) or thematically (discussing sources comparatively in relation to a series of themes or concepts)?
- Which points constitute major landmarks in the essay and which are simply clarifications or examples which fall within the scope of larger points?
- Are there any important aspects of my discussion which don't seem to fit with the other points I want to make? How might I resolve this?
- What can I exclude altogether as irrelevant?

Threading your argument

While your essay might make multiple points and consider a number of different examples, there should nevertheless be a guiding thread linking these together. This thread should be a central argument which acts as a sort of umbrella for all the

> **QUICK TIP**
>
> Talk through your plan with a friend. If your argument doesn't make sense it will become clear when you try to explain it to someone else.

other points you want to make. Don't leave it until the conclusion of your essay to decide what this is: you need to state your central argument in the introduction and support this argument throughout.

The thread is usually a variation of the essay question. For example, with the above example on media, the central argument would consist of identifying the multiple roles played by the media in society. However, where the question set is particularly vague or open-ended, it is important to establish early on how **you** understand this question and how **you** intend to engage with it. Consequently, your central line of argument might challenge or criticise some of the concepts or terms introduced by the essay question. For example, you might want to demonstrate the limitations of using a generic term like 'media' to cover a whole range of different technologies and forms of communication. Likewise, if a question requires you to argue for and against a certain position, you might want to show the limitations of setting up two opposing positions to deal with a complex topic or issue.

QUICK TIP

Use this central thread to link the various sections of your essay together. It should always be easy to bring your discussion back to this guiding principle. If not, you have digressed too far from the focus of the essay.

Point – Example – Explanation (P.E.E.) structure

This is a well-known formula, popular with secondary school teachers, which is worth revisiting when planning your essay. Although it imposes a fairly rigid structure onto essay writing, it is a useful tool if you have a tendency to waffle, just tell stories or generally miss the point. While it is used in schools to help children structure their paragraphs, you can also apply it to larger sections of writing or even an entire essay. Here's a breakdown.

- **Point** – the specific concept, idea or argument you will be discussing. State this as clearly as possible.
- **Example** – a clarification of the point. While you may need to go into detail here to explain exactly how this example demonstrates the point, keep this focused. Don't include irrelevant details such as the lengthy background to a study or experiment. Likewise, don't spend too long describing what happens in a literary text or historical event. This is storytelling and should be avoided.

- **Explanation** – this is where you offer an analysis or assessment of the specific value of the point within the wider discussion. It is here that you relate the point back to the central thread of your argument, at the same time indicating how this will be developed or contradicted by a subsequent point.

An example of P.E.E.

> " *Discuss the relationship between literature and the society in which it is produced.* "

1. According to Karl Marx, the 'economic base determines the superstructure'. This means that culture, politics and beliefs are dependent upon current modes of economic production such as manufacturing. **(Point)**

2. For example, the way literature is written and read is dependent upon technology. The rise of the novel in the eighteenth century is linked to the development of cheap mass printing techniques. **(Example)**

3. Consequently, it is important to consider art and literature in relation to the historical context in which they were produced. **(Explanation)**

Make writing up your essay as straightforward as possible by incorporating **P.E.E.** into some or all aspects of your plan.

Different essay models

To develop your essay structure beyond the P.E.E. approach outlined above, it might be helpful to base your essay on existing models. Outlined below are two common models for writing an essay.

Tripartite structure (or the five-paragraph essay)

This is the most common essay structure. It involves presenting two opposed arguments or positions in turn before attempting to reconcile, resolve or find a point of compromise between them. An essay based on this structure can be divided up into five parts:

1. introduction

2. thesis – the first position

3. antithesis – the opposed position

4. synthesis – a resolution of thesis and antithesis

5. conclusion.

An example of tripartite structure

> **"** *Freedom of speech should be protected at all costs. Discuss.* **"**

1. Introduction – With the advent of global and ubiquitous media such as the internet, the issue of freedom of speech has become more important.

2. Thesis – Freedom of speech gives every individual the right to express their opinion and speak out against oppressive treatment and regimes.

3. **Antithesis** – Freedom of speech is dangerous. Children need to be protected from potentially harmful language and images. Language which incites hate and violence should be regulated.

4. **Synthesis** – Freedom of speech should be upheld except when the rights and safety of groups and individuals are put at risk.

5. **Conclusion** – Freedom of speech is a complex issue which cannot be considered independently of other rights.

While this is the simplest and most effective way of organising an essay it can also result in 'sitting on the fence' – a lacklustre essay with no sustained conviction in either of the positions presented.

The polemic structure

The polemic differs from the tripartite structure in that you focus on presenting one argument as forcefully and convincingly as you can, whilst efficiently and effectively dismissing any opposing perspectives. The advantage of this approach is that it commits to one position from the outset. Done well, this can result in a lively essay which demonstrates that the writer has the confidence and skill to follow an argument through. However, to achieve this you need to combine strong rhetoric with clear arguments backed up with powerful examples. Don't rant!

An example of polemic structure

> ❝ *Make a case for the legalisation of soft drugs.* ❞

- **Introduction** – Definition of 'soft' drugs. Brief account of current legislation.

31

- **Argument 1** – Legalisation would allow for regulation and control of substances.
- **Argument 2** – Drug-related crime would be reduced.
- **Argument 3** – Valuable police time and resources spent dealing with dealers and users could be spent dealing with more serious and violent offences.
- **Argument 4** – Allowing the general public easier access to certain 'soft' drugs could lead to a more relaxed society!
- **Conclusion** – Legalisation of soft drugs provides economic and social benefits to the entire population.

QUICK TIP

Choose an essay structure based on what works best for the points you want to make. Some subjects demand a certain format, so make sure you read up on this in your course handbook before you start planning. Equally, as mentioned in Chapter 2, the format of the essay may be indicated by the question itself, if it is structured into several parts.

Tips for top scores

■ Destroy weak links. When writing your plan, avoid linking your points using tangential or over-simplistic links. Think about how all the main points relate to one another and decide upon the best order in which to introduce them so that there is a sense of development rather than simple listing. The stronger the links, the stronger the essay.

■ Don't be afraid to put your cards on the table. To get top marks you need to be prepared to be adventurous and not shy away from expressing an opinion. This might seem risky, but it will pay off if you have plenty of evidence to back you up!

✓ Dos	✗ Don'ts
✓ Return to your essay plan after a good night's sleep.	✗ Leave planning until the last minute.
✓ Test your argument during the planning stage.	✗ Assume a list of loosely related ideas constitutes a plan.
✓ Regularly refer back to your plan and use P.E.E. if you are starting to digress.	✗ Be afraid to argue for one position over another.

PART 2

Writing your essay

So you've done your background reading and organised your ideas into a coherent plan. Now it's time to write up your essay. Over the next three chapters, we will look at how to transform your plan into an intelligent and inspiring piece of writing. We'll be focusing on key components of the essay such as the introduction and conclusion, how to maintain a strong argument throughout, as well as ways to ensure your writing is both exciting and enjoyable to read at the same time as adopting an appropriate academic register.

4 Beginnings and endings

First impressions last. So do last impressions. The introduction and conclusion provide a frame for the essay itself and play an essential role in guiding the reader through your argument. Consequently, they have the power to both seduce and disappoint a reader. A lacklustre introduction doesn't inspire the reader to carry on. An unimaginative conclusion will overshadow the rest of an essay, no matter how brilliant other aspects of your argument might have been. On the other hand, whoever is marking your essay is far more likely to forgive minor weaknesses in the body of the essay if it begins and ends strongly.

QUICK TIP

The first few paragraphs are always the hardest to set down and often sound stilted and awkward. Write your introduction once you have got into your writing 'groove' and it will sound more confident, flow better and convince your reader that you are fully in control of your argument.

Different approaches to writing your introduction

There is no set formula for writing an introduction. Depending on the specific requirements of your course, there may be certain conventions you are expected to follow when introducing your argument. For example, for a science-related essay, you may be expected to begin with a clear statement of a specific problem and how you plan to solve it. For an arts or humanities subject, you might be expected to provide a short outline of the concepts, terms or themes you will be discussing.

We are going to consider three different approaches to writing introductions:

1. contextual

2. conceptual

3. anecdotal.

These approaches are not meant to be all-inclusive but rather provide a starting point for developing your own style and approach to writing introductions.

A contextual approach

A contextual approach situates the discussion topic within a broader context. This context might be socio-historical, political, biographical or theoretical. A biographical context would involve consideration of an author's professional or even personal background.

Example 1 – An essay on representations of gender in the work of Jane Austen might begin with an account of the author's biographical background:

> **"** *As an unmarried female author, Jane Austen's own circumstances provide useful insight into key questions concerning the role and perception of women by women at the end of the 18th century.* **"**

Example 2 – An essay on recent developments in research on the HIV virus could begin by situating these in developments made over the past 30 years:

> **“** *Since the outbreak of the HIV epidemic in the USA and Europe in the early 1980s, research on the virus is marked by a series of major milestones, from the identification of the retrovirus by Gallo and the Pasteur Institute in 1983, to the development, approval and criticism of the drug AZT.* **”**

Merits of this approach:

- works best with longer essays and dissertations (over 3,000 words)
- provides the reader with some background to your argument
- shows awareness of wider implications of your argument and subject matter.

Pitfalls of this approach:

- too much background information can be boring and slow your essay down
- for shorter essays you may not have room for a long contextual introduction.

A conceptual approach

A conceptual approach begins by clearly setting out and defining the concepts and terms you will be using to structure your argument.

Example 1 – Returning to the example of gender representation in Austen, a conceptual approach would involve an explanation and definition of the theoretical framework (e.g. Marxist, feminist, psychoanalytical, etc.) you will be employing to explore the question of gender:

> *" Using Marxist conceptions, this essay will explore how gender relations are determined by social class in Jane Austen's* Emma. *"*

Example 2 – For an essay on research into the HIV virus, a conceptual approach would introduce and explain key concepts or methods used in current research:

> *" Mapping the structure of genomes is essential to our understanding of how different organisms function. A genome map is less detailed than genome sequencing as it just identifies the landmarks rather than listing the order of every DNA or RNA base in a genome. This essay will assess the recent use of the technique known as SHAPE by researchers at Chapel Hill to produce an aerial view of the entire structure of the HIV-1 genome. "*

Merits of this approach:

- works well for shorter essays (under 3,000 words)
- gets straight to the heart of what your essay is about
- avoids confusion later on by defining terms from the outset.

Pitfalls of this approach:

- using purely conceptual language can appear too abstract or vague (especially for humanities essays). Make sure you provide some reference to the specific objects or texts you will be conceptualising

■ you need to avoid defining obvious terms or simply citing dictionary (or, worse, Wikipedia) definitions as this is tedious and adds little value.

An anecdotal approach

No, we don't mean those boring, pointless and seemingly endless stories your uncle tells at family gatherings; an anecdotal approach to writing an essay introduction involves choosing a key quotation or example as a way to open up your discussion. Where a conceptual approach begins by defining terms before applying them to a specific text or phenomenon, an anecdotal approach starts with the details and works outwards.

Example 1 – For our Jane Austen essay, we might begin with a close reading of a key scene from *Emma* in order to raise more general questions about gender representation in Austen's texts:

> **❝** *In describing the first meeting of Emma Woodhouse and Harriet Smith, Austen describes Harriet as possessing a beauty which 'happened to be of a sort which Emma particularly admired'. Emma's subsequent interference in Harriet's love life is just one of several ways in which women are objectified not only by men but also by women during the novel. This essay will consider the ways in which the various women in* Emma *frequently reinforce male discourses which 'objectify' and subordinate them as the 'weaker sex'.* **❞**

Example 2 – The essay on HIV research could open with a recent case study or the identification of new and more virulent strains of the virus in order to emphasise what is at stake for contemporary research:

> ❝ *According to a recent study reported in the* American Journal of Transplantation, *organs infected with the HIV virus should be made available to those suffering with the virus and in desperate need of transplant surgery. In the USA alone this could lead to up to 500 extra donors each year. This demonstrates a notable shift in how the HIV virus is perceived by the medical community and wider public. This essay will consider how recent research on the virus is both shaping and shaped by this change in attitude.* ❞

Merits of this approach:

- works best with longer essays (more than 3,000 words)
- the right quotation, example or case study can provide an exciting and original way to introduce your discussion
- enables you to establish a strong narrative to lead into the main body of your essay.

Pitfalls of this approach:

- avoid simple storytelling – your anecdote must ultimately make an important and relevant point
- be careful your anecdote doesn't take over your entire essay. Make sure that you also engage with the larger issues and concepts raised by the question.

Choose the approach which you think best grabs the attention of your reader before leading naturally into a clear outline of the argument and points you will be developing in the essay itself.

QUICK TIP

Writing or revising your introduction at the end of the essay writing process can be an extremely useful exercise, particularly for longer essays, projects and dissertations.

Ask yourself the following.

- Have you done what you set out to do?
- Has your essay taken a slightly different direction from the one originally proposed?
- Don't write your essay to fit your introduction, but make sure your introduction fits your essay by writing it when you have finished the rest of your essay.

Powerful conclusions

A conclusion should suggest the outcome of a discussion or argument. If it simply repeats the questions posed at the start of the essay, the implication is that the pages in between have done little to develop the discussion. Readers, especially those with red pens, want an easy life. They don't want to have to reread an essay several times in order to work out what the author was actually trying to say. A powerful conclusion shows you have achieved what you set out to do and gives the reader something to think about.

A conclusion is the most important part of any piece of academic study and consequently everything else in your essay should work towards this crowning moment. It makes sense, therefore, that you begin here. While this approach seems to go against our instincts to begin at the beginning, having a very well-defined idea of where you want to end up at the close of your essay can provide your writing with an extremely powerful driving force. Having some detailed notes or even a set of statements you want to include in your conclusion and referring to these regularly can be very useful as you develop your argument.

Summarise, don't repeat

Your conclusion should bring together different elements of your argument. This may involve a small amount of summarising, but it should never simply be a repetition of:

- the essay question
- the introduction or
- aspects of your argument.

Equally, suggesting how your discussion has wider implications or raises further questions will demonstrate an awareness of the wider context in which your argument is situated. For example, having discussed current research on the HIV virus, you might suggest areas which remain unexplored or which you envisage becoming more prominent in the future. However, you should avoid introducing new material or points which refer to the existing argument.

Sitting on the fence

When concluding you need to put your cards firmly on the table. Hedging your bets in your conclusion suggests a lack of confidence in the arguments you have presented. Even if your analysis and discussion do not lead to any definitive answers, your conclusion still needs to be conclusive. Before settling for a wishy-washy conclusion, think about why you have failed to come down on one side or the other. Do you need to go back and revise your argument? If you are working with data or case studies, does the lack of concrete answers attest to unforeseen methodological problems or suggest the need for further enquiries? Perhaps the essay question itself doesn't lend itself to a definitive answer, in which case you might raise this as an issue in your conclusion. However, avoid sounding arrogant here as you may risk irritating or offending the person who set the question in the first place!

How not to write a conclusion

Some of the worst writing appears in essay conclusions. This is partly because students tend to run out of time, but it's also due to an uncertainty about how to formulate this section of the essay. Below are some classic examples of what **not** to say in your conclusion.

1. 'I think that I have shown . . .', followed by a regurgitation of the essay title. This approach lacks confidence and suggests you are not entirely sure you have done what you set out to do. If you're not convinced, your reader won't be either. Don't **think** it: **do** it, then **say** it.

2. 'As the above discussion demonstrates, there are both positive and negative elements to consider. On the one hand . . . on the other hand . . .' Avoid platitudes. Even when it's difficult to offer a definitive outcome to your enquiry, your conclusion should not be a copy and paste job.

3. 'Another argument we could have considered . . .' Don't bring in new material, especially not to lament its absence from the main body of your essay. Include it there or leave it out.

4. 'By way of conclusion, I would like to end with the following quotation: . . .' This is a cop-out and not a real conclusion. Avoid using quotations in place of clearly expressing the outcome of your argument or investigation.

QUICK TIP

There is no rule about how long or short your introduction and conclusion need to be. What is important is that they are well thought out and relevant to the essay question. One suggested rule of thumb is that your introduction and conclusion should both be somewhere between a tenth and a sixth of the total word count. Any longer and they will overwhelm the essay and prevent you from adequately developing your actual argument. Any shorter and they risk sounding superficial and purely perfunctory, or just there for the sake of it.

Tips for top scores

■ Identify the limitations of the essay question. How does it restrict the conclusions that can be drawn? How might it be rephrased to broaden the scope of the discussion?

■ In drawing your own conclusions, make it clear how you have moved the debate forward during the essay. This involves looking back at what you have **done** over the course of the essay rather than simply thinking about what you have **shown**. For example, applying certain concepts to a literary text does not simply demonstrate certain points about the text but demonstrates the validity of using this type of methodology to carry out research.

✓ **Dos**	✗ **Don'ts**
Introductions	
✓ Engage directly with the question.	✗ Include irrelevant or over-general material not closely linked to the essay itself.
✓ Explain your terms clearly and concisely.	✗ Use the introduction to stall beginning the essay itself.
✓ Inspire your reader to keep reading.	✗ Include too much detail or analysis that should be saved for the body of the essay.
Conclusions	
✓ Show how you have answered the essay question.	✗ Simply repeat either the essay question or introduction.
✓ Suggest the wider implications of the discussion.	✗ Run out of space and tack on a two-line conclusion as an afterthought.
✓ Leave the reader with something to think about.	✗ Introduce new points or material which should have been dealt with in the body of the essay.

5 Making your point

Transforming a series of brief bullet points and sub-headings into a clearly structured, easy-to-follow argument is often easier said than done. Be prepared to revise your plan as you write up your essay in order to make your argument as strong as possible.

Signposting your argument

Just because the points you want to make seem obvious to you doesn't mean they will make sense to anyone else. You need to gently guide your reader through your argument, spelling out the connections between each point.

Think of your essay as a journey of discovery. Your reader needs to know where they are going, where they have been and why. Throughout your essay be sure to include signposts – markers which remind your reader of where they are in your argument, how this relates back to the opening question and where you will be taking them next.

Signposts can take the form of a single sentence or short paragraph.

- 'In order to evaluate the various methods outlined above, I will consider each in turn with reference to a series of case studies.'
- 'In addition to the economic and environmental issues discussed above, our analysis also raises a number of further questions

concerning the social and cultural impact of car ownership. These will be discussed in detail in the following section.'

Signposts are particularly important following a lengthy example or case study which may have taken the discussion away from the central argument.

Don't make your signposting too obvious or laboured. Your signposting should be worked into the fabric of the essay. Avoid being too repetitive (e.g. 'I will do this, then I will do this, then I will do this . . .'). You might consider using rhetorical questions as a way of signposting:

> **❝** *Although Smith has presented us with a very convincing argument, might there be another way of approaching the question?* **❞**

However, be careful not to overdo this as using too many rhetorical questions sounds contrived and risks irritating the reader.

Using signposts in the development of your argument

Be careful not to substitute signposts for genuine development of your argument. Consider the following series of events.

1. Wake up.

2. Get out of bed.

3. Brush teeth.

Each event follows on from the previous one. Now let's add signposts:

Having *woken up*, *I* will now *get out of bed* before proceeding to *brush my teeth*.

But what if we mixed up the order?

Having *brushed my teeth*, *I* will now *get up* before proceeding to *wake up*.

It's easy to see that the order doesn't make sense, despite the signposts used. The same applies to the information you present in your essay. Not only should it be presented in a logical order, but each subsequent point should usually relate closely to the previous one.

Avoiding the strawmen

A strawman argument involves constructing a very weak, flimsy argument (the strawman) in order to knock it down, thus demonstrating your intellectual prowess. Strawmen might include:

- theories which have long been discredited (e.g. Aristotle's theory of gravity)
- overly simplistic readings of a primary source (e.g. the view that C.S. Lewis's *The Lion, the Witch and the Wardrobe* is just a book about a lion, a witch and a wardrobe)
- non-academic opinions (e.g. those offered in newspapers or online news sources).

> **QUICK TIP**
> This is not to say that the above examples should never be employed:
> an essay on the history of theories of gravity would no doubt require a
> discussion of Aristotle. You should simply avoid using them as if they were
> key arguments just because they are easy to criticise.

While it is important that you show the ability to criticise existing arguments and ideas, there is no point doing this with an argument no one takes seriously. You won't be awarded marks for this. It also takes up valuable space in your essay which could be used to develop a more convincing argument. To be a heavyweight you need to face serious opponents.

Irrelevant criticisms

Similarly, when presenting various objections to an argument, theory or scientific method, ask yourself whether these criticisms seriously challenge the validity of the argument or approach. Presenting superficial or irrelevant criticisms can make you look as though you have missed the point. Consequently, it is far better to demonstrate a thorough understanding of a particular theory or argument without necessarily launching an attack on it.

Strawmen from secondary literature

If you have trouble formulating your own criticisms or objections, consulting secondary literature might help. However, don't lower your guard as academic publications are full of strawmen. Replicating the poor arguments made by others is as bad, if not worse, than coming up with your own strawmen!

Selecting quotations and examples

Every point you make, no matter how minor, should be backed up with evidence. This might simply be an additional sentence which clarifies exactly what you mean, a quotation from a key source, a brief reference to a well-known example or a detailed case study. It is important to remember that the quotations and examples you use to illustrate your argument do just that.

Don't let examples and quotations take over your essay! Only use a quotation or example if it supports your own point; don't use it to make a point for you.

Quotations

To make the best possible use of the quotations you have gathered, ask yourself the following questions.

❝ *Do I need to include a quotation here?* **❞**

Does the quotation clarify and back up the statement or explanation you have given? Does it simply duplicate information you have already provided? Make sure that you do not use a quotation to avoid having to explain a difficult concept in your own words.

❝ *There are several quotations I could use here: which one should I choose?* **❞**

Choose the quotation which sums up the point you are making as concisely and clearly as possible. Too many long quotations can prevent you adequately expressing your own ideas.

❝ *Should I embed the quotation in my own writing or section it off?* **❞**

A key phrase or term can be worked into your own sentence, e.g. 'Jeremy Bentham's concept of "the greatest good for the greatest number" places the interests of the group above those of each individual.'

But be careful not to simply **join the dots** between a series of quotations. For example:

> " *According to Sigmund Freud, 'under the influence of the ego's instincts of self-preservation, the pleasure principle is replaced by the reality principle'. This means that 'This latter principle does not abandon the intention of ultimately obtaining pleasure, but it nevertheless demands and carries into effect the postponement of satisfaction,' which also involves 'the abandonment of a number of possibilities of gaining satisfaction and the temporary toleration of unpleasure as a step on the long indirect road to pleasure'.* "

Here, all I have done is 'frame' a very long quotation using a series of connectives: *'According to'. . . 'This means that'. . . 'which also involves . . .'* without explaining what the quotation actually means. This is an easy trap to fall into and sets off alarm bells as to how much you actually understand of what you're citing. Never include a quotation you haven't properly explained.

Examples

To make the best possible use of the examples you have gathered, ask yourself the following questions.

> " *Will the introduction of an example at this point disrupt the flow of my argument?* "

If the example is relevant and focused, it should clarify rather than disrupt your discussion. However, if the example needs lengthy explanation and raises more than one of the points you want to make, it might be better to introduce it once all these points have been established. You could also refer to it in a footnote, but be careful not to overdo this (see Chapter 7).

> ❝ *Can I allude to an example briefly (in a couple of sentences) or does it need more clarification?* ❞

Although it is often important to include detailed examples or case studies to back up your argument or test a thesis, you can also use brief examples as a way of introducing or explaining individual points or concepts. For example, 'As events such as 9/11 demonstrate, the relationship between religion and politics is more complex than Western governments would like to believe.' Here the reference to 9/11 is well known, so it can highlight the importance or relevance of an issue without needing in-depth explanation.

> ❝ *How can I keep my example as concise as possible without over-simplifying it?* ❞

Decide what is most useful about the example, the details you need to mention and what you can cut out. Keep your eye on the argument at all times. This can be tricky as sometimes the most exciting part of an example, anecdote or case study is actually irrelevant to the point you want to make, but if it's not relevant, don't include it. Don't simply exclude any factors or other bits of information which might be problematic. Instead, allude to these as potential limitations rather than ignoring them altogether.

Tips for top scores

- Use quotations sparingly. You will get significant credit for showing the ability to explain complex ideas and concepts in your own words (obviously referencing your sources). Equally, allocating too much space to quotation will reduce the space you have to develop your own discussion.

■ Find your own examples. Don't rely on the ones given to you in class or offered in textbooks. Prove you really understand something by explaining it with reference to examples or case studies you have identified yourself. This will also demonstrate strong research skills.

■ Choose topical examples. Reading recent editions of academic journals as well as magazines such as *The Economist* or *London Review of Books* will provide you with more recent and relevant examples than those offered in textbooks. Demonstrate your ability to engage with contemporary debates as well as think about the current relevance of a particular topic.

✓ Dos	✗ Don'ts
✓ Make the structure of your argument clear to your reader throughout your essay.	✗ Assume your argument will appear as logical to others as it does to you.
✓ Consult secondary literature to help formulate a valid critique.	✗ Substitute 'signposts' for well-explained connections between points.
✓ Back up your statements with quotations and examples.	✗ Set up strawmen arguments.
	✗ Allow quotations and examples to take over your essay.

6 Writing with style

In the previous chapter, we focused on how to get your point across by clearly organising your argument and examples. However, good organisation isn't the only thing you need to convey your message and achieve top marks; you also need to ensure that your ideas are expressed well. In this chapter, we will look at how you can improve your writing technique and give you tips on how to make your essay a pleasure, not a struggle, to read.

Developing a strong narrative

Sentences and paragraphs work like building blocks. There shouldn't be any gaps between one block and the next or the whole structure of your argument is at risk of collapsing. Therefore, don't try to achieve too much in each sentence or paragraph but take your time building your narrative. Each sentence should only ever include one idea or make one statement. If necessary it should be followed by an example or quotation. Consider the following.

> **Example 1** – *'The Boston Tea Party was a protest against the British government and the East India Company, calling into question the company's monopoly on importing tea into the colonies and creating a legacy of political protest most recently embodied in the Tea Party movements protesting against President Obama's stimulus package.'*

In this example too many ideas are referred to at once and not enough time is spent exploring each in turn.

Example 2 – 'The Boston Tea Party was a protest carried out against the British government and the East India Company which involved dumping three shiploads of taxed tea into Boston harbour. The protest called into question the right of the British government to tax the colonies as a means of raising revenue. It was also part of a larger controversy surrounding the control exercised by the British parliament over British colonies without any elected representation. Consequently, it is considered to be one of the main events leading up to the American Revolution and continues to act as an important reference in contemporary US politics today.'

In this paragraph, the historical importance of the event is explained in more detail before indicating subsequent discussion of contemporary relevance.

Look over each paragraph carefully before moving to the next. Does each sentence add something new? How does every additional sentence move the discussion forward? It is easy to end up saying the same thing two or three times using different language. No matter how well-phrased this 'rephrasing' might be, it is still waffle!

Shorter sentences

To help untangle your ideas, try using shorter sentences wherever possible. A short sentence can be very powerful when used either to introduce or to conclude a paragraph. They can also provide a welcome respite following long, complicated sentences. Use them for the statements you want to emphasise as being important.

Example 1 – 'According to the philosopher Friedrich Nietzsche, "God is dead".'

There is nothing wrong with this sentence, but it lacks energy and the power of the statement made by Nietzsche is diluted.

> **Example 2** – '"God is dead." This is the claim made by Nietzsche in The Gay Science.'

Here the main statement is put into the foreground and isolated from subsequent discussion, giving the reader the chance to appreciate its power and significance before moving on to its contextualisation.

Good and bad writing

Writing is a very personal activity. It can take years of practice to develop a style you are happy with and which is appropriate to the medium you are working in. Don't get frustrated if you haven't yet found your style. There is a lot you can do to improve your technique. Below is a selection of different types of classic 'bad' writing. Avoid these and your writing will improve enormously.

Repetition

A good plan should help you avoid repeating ideas and points, but you also need to watch out for repetitive writing. Do you phrase all your questions in the same way? (For example, 'How should we define . . .?' 'What are the consequences of . . .? 'To what extent does this . . .?' 'What is at stake here?') Do you always use the same words and connectives (however, furthermore, moreover . . .)?

Try substituting your favourite connectives with others. Using a thesaurus can help, but don't use a substitute unless you are sure it works.

You can also try shifting the position of the connective:

> *'However, there are various cases where side effects have occurred.'*

Change to:

> *'There are, however, various cases where side effects have occurred.'*

But watch out for awkward syntax:

> *'There are various cases where side-effects have occurred, however.'*

Note the awkward positioning of 'however'.

Over-familiar, conversational tone

Using the appropriate register is essential to essay writing. In addition to using technical and scientific terms correctly, you need to write like an expert, not as though you're chatting on the phone or in the pub. This doesn't mean you have to use longer words or more complicated syntax than you would in conversation; you just have to avoid slang and colloquial language.

For example:

- *'As I told you before'* → *'As mentioned earlier'*
- *'The results seem okay'* → *'The results appear satisfactory'*
- *'Hamlet went crazy when his mother shacked up with his uncle'* → *'Hamlet was traumatised by the incestuous relationship between his mother and his uncle'*

Using 'I' in essays

How personal is too personal? It is fine to refer to yourself as 'I' when stating what you are setting out to do, but don't take this as an invitation to use a personal tone. Consider the following:

> **"** *I will discuss the various techniques used in data mining before considering their implications.* **"**

> **"** *I will try to explain the various techniques used in data mining before telling you about their implications.* **"**

The above sentences give us the same information but the tone is completely different. The first demonstrates confidence about how to approach the essay. The second has a more personal tone and suggests an uncertainty about what the writer is going to do.

Too much jargon

You are expected to use a certain amount of jargon – appropriate technical, scientific or philosophical language which relates to the subject you study. But avoid showing off. Don't throw in terms you don't fully understand or use terms which belong to a different academic register. This won't impress your reader – especially if you get them wrong. For example:

> **"** *The author engages in a form of writing which embodies a neo-Deleuzian rhizomatic deterritorialisation as she sets out to deconstruct existing ontological paradigms.* **"**

What does this actually mean?

Awkward syntax

Of all the grammatical errors you can make, awkward syntax can be one of the most damaging to your writing style. The most common areas for awkward syntax include the following.

Rhetorical questions

These should be short and punchy. They tend not to work too well if there are multiple questions and/or clauses. Limit each question to one clause.

> ❝ *What are the consequences of these results for short-term policy making and will they lead to further implications including questions about how taxes are levied in certain countries?* ❞

Change to:

> ❝ *What are the consequences of these results for short-term policy making? What are their wider implications? Do they, for example, raise further questions about how taxes are levied in certain countries?* ❞

Embedded quotations

The grammar and syntax linking your prose to the quoted text should be seamless. Don't tie yourself in knots trying to 'tweak' the quotation or your own language to make it all fit. Simply introduce the quotation as a separate bit of text.

> ❝ *Confucius described intelligence as belonging to someone who avoids letting 'slander that gradually soaks into the mind, nor statements that startle like a wound in the flesh'.* ❞

Here the phrasing doesn't make sense in two places:

1. 'that gradually soaks into the mind' – indicates a sub-clause which requires a main clause to complete the sentence

2. 'nor statements' – requires the introduction of a negative construction around the first noun, i.e. 'slander'.

Instead, include the quotation in its entirety before explaining what it means:

> **❝** *According to Confucius: 'He with whom neither slander that gradually soaks into the mind, nor statements that startle like a wound in the flesh, are successful may be called intelligent indeed.' What he means here is that genuine intelligence lies in the ability not to be affected by false and malicious claims or comments intended to hurt and shock.* **❞**

The passive voice

There are numerous reasons why the passive voice is used instead of the active voice. Most notably it shifts the focus from the subject (person or thing doing the action) to the object (person or thing having the action done to them). However, the passive can significantly lengthen a sentence and the risk is that it will result in convoluted, weak prose. Consider the following.

1. 'The government introduced new taxes on petrol in 2008' – active (the focus is on the 'government' as the subject).
   'New taxes on petrol were introduced in 2008' – passive (the focus is on 'new taxes' as object. Here, 'government' has been dropped as irrelevant/implied).

2. 'Smith has raised a number of key objections to Brown's theory' – active (the focus is on Smith as the subject).

'A number of key objections to Brown's theory have been raised by Smith' – passive (here, you cannot drop the subject (Smith), meaning that the passive formulation is longer and clumsier than the active formulation. Even if the main focus of your discussion will be the' objections' and not 'Smith', it is better to keep the active formulation).

QUICK TIP

If you're unsure about other aspects of English grammar and spelling, ask someone with good English to read over your work. Most universities offer workshops for overseas students on English for academic purposes and will also provide help for home students who are struggling.

Unnecessarily long sentences and paragraphs

Keep a tight rein on your sentences and paragraphs. If they start getting too long, you risk compromising the organisation of your argument. If you end up with a sentence which exceeds 60 words, read through it carefully to see if:

- it actually makes sense
- there is any surplus information which can be omitted or
- you can break it up into two (even three) shorter sentences.

For example:

    ❝ *Soil erosion occurs when soil is blown away by the wind or washed away by heavy rainfall and is often found in areas with steep slopes, widespread deforestation and overpopulation such as Nepal, situated in the Himalayan mountains, which experiences severe problems caused by soil erosion due to its rapidly increasing population, but which can nevertheless be reduced through the use of irrigation and reforestation techniques together with*

> *the introduction of farming methods which avoid damaging the structure of the soil.* "

Here there are too many sub-clauses and points which need to be broken down. Change to:

> " *Soil erosion occurs when soil is blown away by the wind or washed away by heavy rainfall. It is often found in areas with steep slopes, widespread deforestation and overpopulation. A well-known example is Nepal, situated in the Himalayan mountains, which experiences severe problems caused by soil erosion due to its rapidly increasing population. Nevertheless, soil erosion can be reduced through the use of irrigation and reforestation techniques together. It is also important to introduce farming methods that avoid damaging the structure of the soil.* "

The pauses introduced with each new sentence makes it easier to follow each point in turn.

Similarly, a paragraph should only ever include one main point along with the necessary explanation and examples/quotation. If you find a paragraph (and the essay) running away with itself, there is a strong chance you are either digressing or have inadvertently moved on to subsequent points without firmly signalling this to your reader. Again, break it up and, if necessary, start again.

Extraneous information

There is always a strong temptation to try to show your reader how much you know about a subject, regardless of whether or not it helps you answer the question. While you might have succeeded in banishing entire paragraphs of irrelevant material, it can sometimes sneak into individual sentences. Be strict here and get rid of anything which might distract your reader from the point you are making. Read through your essay once you've finished, crossing out anything that is irrelevant.

Consider the following examples.

- *'Charles Darwin was a British naturalist who published* On the Origin of Species *in 1859 aged 45.'*
- *'Published in 1859, Darwin's* On the Origin of Species *was one of the first major studies of natural selection and evolution.'*

In the first example, it is unclear whether the writer is providing a historical biography of Charles Darwin or introducing a discussion on his text. In the second example, it is clear that the writer is interested in discussing the importance of Darwin's study of evolution.

Tips for top scores

- Add energy. If you're happy that you've developed a strong, interesting line of argument, start thinking how you can enhance this further through your writing style. Take cues from published academic writers. How do they keep the reader interested? What type of phrasing or rhetoric do they employ? Developing your own writing style is about emulating (not imitating) writing that inspires you.

- Be confident without being arrogant. There is a fine line between showing that you are in complete control of your material and coming across as cocky. Avoid overburdening your essay with rhetoric which isn't backed up with solid evidence. While the occasional use of irony can add some energy to your essay, don't try to show off by including silly jokes or sarcastic comments.

✓ Dos	✗ Don'ts
✓ Get to the point.	✗ Include too much information in one sentence or paragraph.
✓ Keep sentences and paragraphs focused.	✗ Repeat yourself.
✓ Vary your connectives.	✗ Use words you don't fully understand.
✓ Adopt an appropriate tone.	
✓ Pay attention to syntax.	

PART 3

Essay presentation

Congratulations! The hardest parts of the essay writing process – planning and writing – are done. Now all you need to do is ensure your essay is well presented and correctly referenced. Although relatively stress-free, this can sometimes be fiddly and more time-consuming than expected. The following chapters will walk you through the various things you need to pay attention to when putting the finishing touches to your essay.

7 References and bibliography

An important aspect of essay writing is the ability to use references appropriately. At undergraduate level, you will be expected to include references, both within your essay and as a bibliography – a list of all works used and cited – at the end of the essay. At best, failure to reference correctly is sloppy, at worst it is tantamount to plagiarism. Any work you cite or paraphrase needs to be clearly indicated. Examiners get extremely irritated by careless referencing. Referencing is not simply a formality: references act as a guide to your reader, indicating where they can find the sources you cite. Incorrect or inconsistent referencing is confusing and suggests there may be further inaccuracies in how you cite and use the work of others.

QUICK TIP

Save time by correctly referencing as you go along rather than leaving it to the end. If you need to return to the library to check on a page number or other detail, highlight the missing information in bold or red so you don't forget.

How to use footnotes and endnotes

A footnote appears at the bottom of the page on which the reference is made. An endnote appears as part of a list of references appearing at the end of the essay. Footnotes and endnotes allow you to include a reference cited in the main body of your essay without interrupting the essay itself. They can also include further details which might be useful to the reader but which would disrupt discussion if included in the body of the essay.

A footnote or endnote reference looks like this:

[1] Susan Sontag, *On Photography* (London: Penguin Books, 1979), p.100.

You should consult your departmental handbook to determine whether there is a preference for using footnotes or endnotes. You should also check the specific format these should take and whether you need to use a certain style guide (explained below). While journal articles and book chapters tend to use

QUICK TIP

Check whether you should or shouldn't include a space in page references, i.e. p.100 or p. 100. Small things like this can save you valuable marks!

endnotes, footnotes are often preferred by those marking essays since it enables them to see straight away whether a citation or point has been referenced correctly without having to turn to the notes at the end.

Author–date referencing

For some subjects (primarily sciences and social sciences), the convention is to use the author–date system of referencing instead of footnotes or endnotes. The author–date reference is inserted into the body of the text following a citation or reference and is limited to the surname of the author, followed by the date of publication plus page number. For example, the footnote reference 'David Brown, *Essays on Time Travel* (New York, NY and London: Penguin, 1999), p.32' would appear as '(Brown: 1999; 32)'.

If there is more than one text published by Brown in 1999 cited in the essay, the year of publication is given the suffix 'a', 'b', 'c', etc., e.g. '(Brown: 1999a; 32)'. Similarly, if more than one author named Brown is cited, the author's initial(s) should also be used. For example, Brown would then be specified as D. Brown.

If you are using author–date referencing, it is important to set out your bibliography first to avoid any unnecessary confusion between authors and publications. Consequently, you should make sure your referencing and bibliography use the same styling.

Style guides: a quick guide

A style guide contains specific rules about how to reference different sources in an academic essay or article. Different style guides are adopted by different academic disciplines. Some common style guides are listed below.

- *APA Style* (6th edition) – the style guide of the American Psychological Association. Uses author–date format and is used in the field of psychology.
- *Chicago Manual of Style* – has options for both author–date and footnote referencing. Widely used in the humanities and some social sciences.
- *Harvard System of Referencing* – uses author–date format and is mostly used by the social sciences.
- *IEEE* – uses a numerical reference in square brackets, e.g. '[5]', which corresponds to a text in a list of numbered references. It is used in engineering and technical sciences.

- *MHRA Style Guide* – published by the Modern Humanities Research Association. Used most widely in the UK in the arts and humanities and is based on footnote referencing.
- *MLA Style Manual* – published by the Modern Languages Association and used in the humanities and, more specifically, the fields of languages and literatures. It is based on author–page rather than author–date citations.
- *OSCOLA* – the *Oxford Standard for Citation of Legal Authorities* – is used in the field of law and legal studies. It is based on footnote referencing.
- *Vancouver Style* – based on rules established by the International Committee of Medical Journal Editors. It uses numerical references in square brackets and is used in the field of medicine and related sciences.

Find out which guide is used by your department and where you can download or purchase a copy. Whatever guide is used, it should provide clear examples of how to format your references, as well as answers to common questions concerning issues such as how you should reference multiple authors, unpublished works or foreign language titles.

> **QUICK TIP**
>
> Check your departmental guide very carefully once you've finished your essay. Avoid losing valuable marks for careless and inconsistent referencing by taking the time to double check.

You should also check whether your department deviates from the standard guide in any way. For example, film, media studies and music departments may have much clearer information on referencing film, television and music than tends to be offered by established style guides.

Abbreviated references

References tend to be included in the word count of an essay whereas the bibliography is not. Therefore, it is important not to use up your word limit by repeating the full details of a reference. For this reason, the author–date format is often considered the most efficient system.

Referencing abbreviations

Short title

After the first reference to a text, you can use an abbreviated version comprising the author's surname, the short title of the text and the specific page reference.

> [3] **Roger Scruton, *Kant: A Very Short Introduction* (Oxford and New York, NY: Oxford University Press, 2001), p. 12.**
>
> . . .
>
> [8] **Scruton, *Kant*, p. 52.**

Ibid.

If a reference is immediately followed by another reference to the same text, the author and title in the second reference can be substituted with *'ibid.'* followed by the page number (if different).

> [7] **Dan Brown, *The Da Vinci Code* (London: Bantam Press, 2003), p.77.**
> [8] ***Ibid.*, p.91.**

Op. cit.

This indicates that a work has been cited before but not in the immediately preceding note.

[5] Dan Brown, *The Da Vinci Code* (London: Bantam Press, 2003), p.77.

[6] Stewart Ferris, *The Key to the Da Vinci Code* (Surrey: Crombie Jardine, 2005), p.101.

[7] Brown, *op. cit.*, p.75.

Et al.
Reference to additional authors.

[32] Philip Kotler *et al., Principles of Marketing* (Harlow: FT Prentice Hall, 2005), p.12.

Ed.
Reference for a single editor; 'eds' refers to multiple editors.

[4]Keith Tester (ed.), *The Flâneur* (London: Routledge, 1994), p.3.

Trans.
Translated by (used when referring to a text originally published in another language).

[1] Michel de Certeau, *The Practice of Everyday Life,* trans. Steven Rendall (Berkeley, CA: University of California Press, 1984), p.9.

Other material included in footnotes and endnotes

Keep footnotes and endnotes to a minimum. Avoid using them to carry out discussions or arguments which don't fit into the main body of your essay. If there is no room or place for these points in the essay itself, they should probably be excluded altogether.

Conversely, if you feel they are important enough to be mentioned, you need to find a way to include them in the essay itself.

Consider the following two examples:

> [1] **Another important point to note here is the one made by Maurice Merleau-Ponty in** *The Phenomenology of Perception,* **trans. Colin Smith (New York, NY: Humanities Press, 1962). Here he claims that 'the body is our general medium for having a world' (p. 169).**

If this is an important point, why is it not included in the essay?

> [2] **Further reading in this field might include Maurice Merleau-Ponty,** *The Phenomenology of Perception,* **trans. Colin Smith (New York, NY: Humanities Press, 1962).**

Here, the writer needs to indicate briefly **why** the reader might want to look at this text, while making it clear why it is not being discussed in the essay. This is the best way to use footnotes and endnotes in your essay.

Setting out your bibliography

A bibliography consists of a list of all of the texts and other sources which have been used in the writing of an essay. Don't try and show off by listing texts you haven't read as your examiner will wonder why they are not mentioned in the essay. If a text has been instrumental in guiding and developing your thought, you need to find a way to reference it, even if only briefly. This will ensure that you do not take the credit for ideas belonging to others and risk being accused of plagiarism.

Your bibliography should be organised in alphabetical order by author surname. If there is more than one publication by the same author, these should be organised by publication date. For subsequent publications it is not necessary to repeat the author's name, which can be substituted with just their surname or '——', for example:

> Deleuze, Gilles, *Nietzsche et la philosophie* (Paris: Presses Universitaires de France, 1962).
> ——, *Logique du sens* (Paris: Minuit, 1969).
> ——, *Foucault* (Paris: Minuit, 1986).

However, if an author has published both single-authored and co-authored texts, these should be treated as separate authors. After the first author of a co-authored text, additional authors should appear as 'first name last name':

> Deleuze, Gilles and Félix Guattari, *Capitalisme et schizophrénie: L'Anti-Œdipe* (Paris: Minuit, 1972).

Where there are more than three co-authors, the first three should be listed followed by '*et al.*':

> Adorno, T.W., Max Horkheimer, Georg Simmel *et al.*, *German Sociology* (London: Continuum, 1997).

If the entry is longer than one line, the additional lines should be indented, as above.

Setting out your bibliography with footnotes/ endnotes

If you have used footnotes or endnotes to reference, you should set out your bibliography as follows.

Books

Author surname, first name, *Title* (City where published: Publisher, Year).

> **Srednicki, Mark,** *Quantum Field Theory* **(Cambridge: Cambridge University Press, 2007).**

Journal articles

Author surname, first name, 'Title of article' in *Journal Name*, Vol:Issue (Year), page range.

> **Blackmond Laskey, Kathryn, 'Quantum physical symbol systems' in** *Journal of Logic, Language and Information,* **15:1–2 (2006), 109–54.**

Your course handbook and style guide should provide you with details of how to reference other sources such as films and online references.

Author–date referencing in the bibliography

If you have used author–date referencing, the publication date requires greater emphasis and you should set out your bibliography as follows.

Books

> **Srednicki, M. (2007),** *Quantum Field Theory,* **Cambridge: Cambridge University Press.**

Journal articles

Blackmond Laskey, K. (2006), 'Quantum physical symbol systems' in *Journal of Logic, Language and Information*, 15:1–2, 109–54.

Using reference management software

For longer essays and dissertations, you might find it helpful to use reference management software such as EndNote or RefWorks. This software acts like a database: you add the full details of each book, article, chapter or other source you use. You then link your Word document to the citation software. This enables you to insert a reference in the correct format into your essay and produce a bibliography without having to type each reference out every time it appears.

However, always make sure the citation software you plan to use supports the specific style guide required by your course.

Tips for top scores

- Where relevant, show sensitivity to the original publication date of a text, which may differ from the edition you are citing. This also applies to texts appearing in translation. This will demonstrate awareness of historical context and help you establish a chronology of different texts and ideas.

■ It is also important to try to cite from editions considered definitive by academics. For example, different religious studies departments will advise students to use a certain edition of the Bible.

■ Use your footnotes to provide evidence of extensive reading beyond those texts which have made it to the main body of your essay. Although you should avoid showing off, examiners appreciate a brief indication that you have considered other critics or examples. You might like to highlight:
  o areas for further reading
  o other researchers, critics or scholars working in the field
  o useful examples which deal with a similar problem or issue.

✓ Dos	✗ Don'ts
✓ Note down full references as you go along.	✗ Carry out lengthy discussions or introduce main points in your footnotes.
✓ Be consistent with your referencing.	✗ Repeat the full reference every time you cite a text.
✓ Check which style guide is used in your department.	✗ Jump between author–date and footnote referencing.
✓ Organise your bibliography in alphabetical order.	

8 Formatting your work

While you are being assessed for what you say, not how pretty your essay looks, good presentation is still crucial. The key here is to be consistent. Decide how you want your essay to look and stick to it.

Using data, graphs and images

Sometimes it is useful or even necessary to illustrate a point using a visual example. Equally, you might be expected to present the results of your investigations in the form of a diagram or graph. As with quotations and examples, it is best to choose a small selection of key images that best exemplify or explain your point. Avoid the temptation to include too many images as they will simply distract and confuse the reader and disrupt the flow of your essay.

Each image (or figure) should be clearly labelled with a figure number and a short title or explanation (plus the name of the artist or photographer if appropriate). The figure number (Fig. 1, Fig. 2, etc.) should be used when referring to the image in the essay. Tables should be labelled Table 1, Table 2, etc.

Example 1

Figure 1. *Riot police on Oxford Street.*
(Photograph used with permission from Sophie Fuggle.)

Example 2

Figures and tables should be inserted into your essay between paragraphs, not between sentences in the same paragraph. They should be inserted as close as possible to the point in the essay where they are being discussed. Try to avoid squashing too much information into a single page or leaving enormous gaps between figures and text.

81

	Male	Female
Meat eating	35	32
Pescatarian (fish only)	23	21
Vegetarian	12	15
Vegan	3	5

Table 1. Results of survey concerning dietary habits of men and women aged 21–35.

Appendices

If you have extensive data you wish to refer to which cannot be reproduced as a few neat diagrams or tables, you could include an appendix at the end of your essay. This provides the reader with a full set of data and/or images from which the essay takes a few key examples. Appendices are not usually included in the word count but it is worth bearing in mind that, like the bibliography, an appendix constitutes an optional reference point for the reader. This means that the person marking your essay might look briefly at the appendix but will not consider it part of the material being assessed. Therefore, if a table or graph is essential to your argument you should try to include it in the main body of your essay.

General essay presentation

Here are some key points about essay presentation to consider.

Fonts: styles and sizes

Use the same font throughout and choose a font that is clear and easy to read. Avoid anything which is difficult to make out, like *Freestyle script*; looks silly, such as **Jokerman**; or heavy, like **impact**.

If you are emailing your essay or submitting it via your university's online learning system, make sure you have chosen a generic (standard) font. Otherwise you risk having the essay default to another standard font which could significantly affect the appearance of your essay. Frequently, the default is **Courier New**, which looks like an old-fashioned typewriter font.

Headings and sub-headings

Unless you are specifically required to do so, avoid using too many headings and sub-headings, especially in a short essay – these will just disrupt the flow of your essay. For an essay of 3,000 words or less there is no reason to include sub-headings unless you want to. Don't use different fonts for headings. Instead put headings in **bold** or *italics* to make them stand out.

If you are expected to use numbered headings and sub-headings (e.g. 1., 1.1., 1.1.1., etc.) you need to establish a coherent system. For example:

1. Some preliminary remarks – bold, 12 pt
1.1. Recent research methods – bold, italics, 12 pt
1.1.1 Lab-based methods – bold, 11 pt
1.1.1.1. Lab-based methods using regional samples – roman, 11 pt

Quotations

As a general rule, quotations which are less than four lines long should be kept in the main body of the text using the same font size and indicated using either "..." or '...'. Check your style guide to see if there is a preference. Be consistent as to whether you use single or double quotation marks.

Quotations (such as speech) within quotations should take the **other** format, i.e. if you use single quotation marks to designate a quotation, the quotation within the quotation should take double quotation marks. For example:

> *'And God said, "Let there be light," and there was light.'*
> *(Genesis 1:3)*

Quotations which are longer than four lines should appear in a separate paragraph. These should not have quotation marks but should be indented and/or formatted in a smaller font size (e.g. 8 pt).

For example:

> *In an essay entitled 'Space versus Program', Bernard Tschumi identifies important parallels between literature and architecture and asks how literary techniques could inform architectural practice:*

>> *If writers could manipulate the structure of stories in the same way as they twist vocabulary and grammar, couldn't architects do the same, organizing the program in a similarly objective, detached, or imaginative way? For if architects could self-consciously use such devices as repetition, distortion, or juxtaposition in the formal elaboration of walls, couldn't they do the same thing in terms of the activities that occurred within those very walls?*

Quoting poetry or lyrics

When quoting poetry or lyrics, you can format your quotations in two ways:

1. Embed it into the text of your essay using '/' to denote new lines, for example: 'Shall I compare thee to a summer's day?/ Thou art more lovely and more temperate.'

2. Format it in a separate paragraph, for example:

   Shall I compare thee to a summer's day?
   Thou art more lovely and more temperate.

Whichever you do, it is vital to retain the original line breaks.

When quoting speech involving more than one character from a play or screenplay, it is also preferable to place this in a separate paragraph in order to maintain the original formatting.

> **QUICK TIP**
>
> Mathematical and scientific formulae should also be indented but should be presented in the same or a slightly larger font size than the main text for clarity.

Try to replicate the quotation exactly as it appears in the original text or source. If there is a term you wish to emphasise, you can put it in italics, but you must indicate this using square brackets, i.e. '[my italics]', after the quotation. Likewise, if you need to replace a pronoun so that the quotation makes sense, put this in square brackets. For example:

   ❝ *He has claimed on numerous occasions that the system would never work.* **❞**

If it is not clear to whom 'He' refers, replace this pronoun as follows:

   ❝ *[Brown] has claimed on numerous occasions that the system would never work.* **❞**

Use of ellipsis

Avoid over-use of ellipsis [. . .] when quoting, as this risks giving the impression that you have taken the quotation out of context. For example, take the following quotation from Friedrich Engels:

> **"** *Communism now no longer meant the concoction, by means of the imagination, of an ideal society as perfect as possible, but insight into the nature, the conditions and the consequent general aims of the struggle waged by the proletariat.* **"**

Consider the distortion of the original quotation through an (exaggerated) over-use of ellipsis:

> **"** *Communism [. . .] meant [. . .] an ideal society [. . .] and the [. . .] aims of [. . .] the proletariat.* **"**

Using italics

Italics should be used sparingly and in the following circumstances.

1. To quote the title of a book (but not a journal article, which should be in regular text, denoted with single quotation marks). The same applies to footnotes and bibliographic references (see Chapter 7).

2. When using a foreign language term which has not been widely accepted into the English language. For example, 'The term *oikos* was used by the Greeks to refer to the sphere of the household.'

3. To highlight key terms, e.g. 'Here we will consider the three main principles upon which a critical rationalist view of science is built: *falsification*, *criticism* and *demarcation*.'

4. To place rhetorical emphasis on a word or phrase. Keep this to a minimum as otherwise it will lose its force and risks sounding irritating. For example, 'It is not a question of *how* but *why*.'

Spelling and grammar

Poor spelling and grammar reflects badly on the writer. Not only does it suggest carelessness but it can cause a reader to lose patience as he or she struggles to work out what you intended to say. Use spell and grammar checkers to flag up any obvious mistakes and typos. Proceed with caution, though, as these offer the most obvious suggestions, which are not necessarily the correct ones. Watch out for autocorrect, especially if your essay includes quotations and references to foreign language texts.

> **QUICK TIP**
>
> Decide whether you are going to use American English or UK English endings. American English uses -ize endings where UK English uses -ise. Be consistent with whichever style you opt for.

Common grammar and spelling mistakes

You should always check you have used the correct option in the following cases.

- Its or it's?
- Where, were, we're or wear?
- There, their or they're?
- Your or you're?

Here are some other points to note.

- Avoid using abbreviated forms such as 'don't' and 'can't' as these can sound too informal.

- Plurals and possessives:
  - 'The girl**'s** bicycle' – denotes possession.
  - 'The girl**s** are riding their bicycles' – denotes plural noun.
  - 'The girl**s'** bicycles' – denotes possession relating to a plural noun.
- Use capital letters for days and months, e.g. Monday, **not** monday.
- Use capital letters for adjectives denoting a country or nationality, e.g. French, **not** french.

Layout and spacing

Be consistent in how you align your text and how you delineate new paragraphs. You should either use a line break or an indent – not both – for a new paragraph.

Make sure your text is evenly spaced throughout your essay. Your reader will find it helpful if you use double or 1.5 spacing. This will also give them room to write their comments and corrections clearly. Your departmental handbook will provide further guidelines on required spacing. Be sure to include page numbers on each page for ease of reference.

Tips for top scores

- Don't simply include an image or diagram as evidence of a point you are making. Analyse the information it presents whilst being critical of its limitations. This will demonstrate the ability not only to present evidence but to actively engage with the methods of collecting and presenting data.

■ While meticulous presentation will not ensure top marks on its own, careless presentation can distract a reader and prevent them fully appreciating the strengths of your argument. Ideally, your presentation should go virtually unnoticed, ensuring that your reader focuses solely on your argument, not your use of fonts or sub-headings.

✓ Dos	✗ Don'ts
✓ Label your figures and tables correctly.	✗ Include unnecessary images or diagrams.
✓ Use font styles and sizes consistently.	✗ Use inappropriate or unusual fonts.
✓ Use spell and grammar check (but with caution).	✗ Go crazy with italics.
	✗ Switch between US and UK English.

9 Developing your technique

One of the keys to strong essay writing is the ability to criticise and reflect on your own work. This will enable you to identify and revise problems and mistakes before handing in your essay, as well as helping to improve your technique over the long term. The final chapter will consider some of the ways you can achieve this.

Effective proofreading

Before submitting your finished essay, make sure you carefully read through your work one last time. Proofreading a recently completed essay can be tricky. It can be easy to miss major typos and omissions because your (tired) brain reads what it thinks should be there rather than **what is actually there**. Here are a few helpful techniques to ensure you proofread your work properly.

- Give yourself a break between writing and rereading your work. If possible, have a good night's sleep to give you enough distance to come back to the essay with fresh eyes.
- Ask someone with an eye for detail to proofread your work. However, to avoid passing off someone else's work as your own (i.e. plagiarism), you should ask them to flag up typos and awkward phrasing. They shouldn't make any corrections for you or rewrite any passages.

- Write a checklist. If you're prone to careless presentation or serious omissions and errors, compile a list of things to check and check each thing off one at a time. Some examples are given below.
  - o **Font size and style** – Are these consistent throughout for body text, quotations and references?
  - o **References** – Does every reference include the correct page number?
  - o **Quotations** – Have you used single or double quotation marks consistently?
- Read your essay aloud. This is possibly the best way of spotting when something is missing, repetitive or doesn't make sense. You can either do this alone or in front of a willing audience. Articulating every word and sentence vocally is far more effective than simply casting your eyes over the text. Remember – if you're not happy saying something out loud, do you really want someone else reading it?

Learning from the process

Once you've submitted an essay, don't think that's the end of the process. Try and learn as much as you can from the experience so that you don't make the same mistakes next time. Make a mental note of any difficulties or problems you had so you can avoid or limit these in future.

Common problems and solutions for future essays

- **Not enough time.** Set aside more time from the outset. Find out key dates and deadlines well in advance so you can clear your schedule beforehand.

- **Difficulty understanding essay title or approach expected.**
Arrange a meeting with your lecturer or tutor well in advance
to talk through any major problems. Come prepared with
specific questions.
- **Lack of resources available.** Get hold of key texts well in
advance. Head to the library the moment the questions are
set. Ask the course convenor before they set the essays to put
limited material on short loan.

Learning from feedback

Feedback from examiners can vary enormously, from detailed
annotations and extensive advice for improvement to a few
basic remarks. Don't be disheartened by harsh criticism or brief
comments. If you haven't achieved the grade you hoped for, try to
build on the experience so that you can improve next time.

- If possible, ask your tutor or lecturer to explain comments or
criticisms.
- Make a note of any suggestions provided, such as increasing
secondary reading, and try to implement these in your next
essay.
- If the feedback flags up any major problems, such as poor
English, take measures to improve these before your next
essay is due. Most universities have study skills centres which
should provide advice and workshops to help you over the long
term.
- Go over your essay again, making reference to the grade
boundary guidelines for your course. Retrospectively, it will
be far easier to see why you have been awarded a certain
grade. Start thinking about what you need to do to move up a
boundary so you can incorporate this directly into how you plan
and write your next essay.

Improving your writing style over the long term

As discussed in Chapter 6, a strong writing style is not something which happens overnight. Expressing your ideas clearly should get easier with every essay you write. However, just as the material you cover in your course builds on earlier topics and methods, with each essay you need to build on existing ideas and techniques. Thinking of writing as an ongoing process will prevent you from panicking each time you have an essay to write. To achieve this, there are various techniques you can employ.

- Look back over earlier essays before embarking on new ones. This will remind you how far you've come and the things you need to improve on.
- Don't try to revolutionise your writing style in one essay. Focus on tweaking little things rather than completely changing your style. To convince your reader, you need to convince yourself first and you will only do that if you write in a way you are comfortable with.
- Don't limit your reading to the work set for you by your lecturers. The more you read, the more extensive your vocabulary and range of expression will become. Read newspapers and current editions of relevant academic journals and magazines. Don't view reading as a passive process but as a way of coming to think critically about how others express their ideas.
- Set up an ongoing exchange with friends where you read and comment on each other's work. It is often easier to notice and learn from others' mistakes than your own.
- Identify your weaknesses. We all have a tendency to resort to bad habits when under time pressure. Developing an awareness of your main faults over the long term will prevent you finding comfort in them when faced with an essay deadline. Whether you tend to repeat yourself, digress or rely too heavily

on quotations to make your point, having a nagging voice in your head or a big sign above your desk can help keep these in check.

Tips for top scores

■ Don't rest on your laurels. If you are already getting marks in the top grade boundary there may still be room for improvement. Positive feedback should give you the confidence to improve your work further, not give you an excuse to slack off. Focus on any negative comments, no matter how minor, as these will give you vital clues as to how to improve your marks even further.

■ Avoid a one-size-fits-all approach. Be prepared to adapt your register and approach according to the module and, where applicable, the expectations of the person marking the essay. While departmental guidelines on grade boundaries give you an indication of what you should include in an essay, you should supplement these with careful consideration of the specific learning outcomes of the module. Understanding the aims of a module should give you a better idea of what skills and knowledge you need to demonstrate in a specific essay.

✓ Dos	✗ Don'ts
✓ Proofread your work.	✗ Get disheartened by criticism.
✓ Use feedback to improve in future.	✗ Ignore major problems or put off dealing with them until the next essay.
✓ Get advice and help where needed.	✗ Change your style dramatically in one essay.

Essay writing Q & A

I have writer's block: what should I do?

Don't panic. Take a complete break away from your desk. Go for a walk or engage in another activity to clear your head. When you return, focus on writing a single paragraph. The first hundred or so words are always the hardest, so take your time and you will pick up speed as you go along. It might also help to disconnect the internet or go somewhere without any interruptions. Another helpful technique can be to set a timer for 10 or 15 minutes and see how much you can write in that time. If 10 minutes seems too long, make it five and build it up.

What should I do if I can't get hold of the books and other texts I need before the essay is due?

Contact your lecturer or tutor as soon as possible as they may be able to help, especially if the problem is due to poor resource management by the department and/or university library. Also get in touch with other students on your course who might be willing to share texts with you. Otherwise, you may have to pay a premium to have a book express delivered or fork out for electronic journal articles and texts. Find out if there are other students in the same boat with whom who you can share the cost (and material).

Can I change my essay title at the last minute?

There is nothing to stop you changing your title at the last minute. However, think very carefully before doing so. Ask yourself if you have enough time to rewrite a strong plan and do the necessary reading.

What should I do if I've asked my lecturer for advice but haven't received as much help as I would like?

At the end of the day, your lecturer can only give you so much advice. They cannot tell you how to write your essay. Think carefully about exactly what you want to ask so as to make the most any appointments you have with them. They should be happy to look at a preliminary essay plan or give you some ideas for further reading, but they cannot do much more than that. However, if you feel your lecturer is being especially unhelpful, speak to your personal tutor or the head of department. If you need further help with research and writing skills, go to see the study skills department at your university or college.

How can I get an extension on my essay deadline?

Don't assume an extension will be granted. Universities have very strict policies and these are often limited to illness (certified by a doctor) which is serious enough to prevent you from studying, or 'extenuating circumstances', which tend to be limited to the death of a close family member. Getting delayed returning from vacation or having issues with your printer are not normally deemed acceptable reasons for granting an extension. Consult your departmental handbook for guidance. If you're still unsure, contact the person responsible for exams in the department as well as your tutor. Lecturers and tutors may not be in a position to grant extensions so it is important to find out who the relevant person is as soon as possible.

Which style guide should I use for my referencing?

Consult your departmental handbook or web page. If it is still unclear, contact your lecturer. If the choice is left to you, choose the referencing style favoured by your discipline (see Chapter 7 for a list).

Can I use a proofreading service to ensure my English is of a good standard?

Check your departmental guidelines on this. Paying someone to read and correct your work is a grey area and policy varies from department to department. In all cases, you should avoid having someone make major revisions to your work as this constitutes plagiarism. Equally, while it is good to have someone point out your mistakes, having someone correct everything for you will prevent you improving your standard of English over time.

Glossary

Abbreviated reference
A short version of a full reference to a text or other work. After the first time a text is referenced, subsequent references should take an abbreviated form.

Anecdote
An example, case or account recounted in order to identify a key point or question.

Appendices
Additional material, such as statistical data, included at the end of an essay, providing clarification of data and examples used in the essay itself.

Argument
A point of view, with supporting premises/evidence, which is intended to persuade others.

Author–date referencing
The author and year of publication appears in parentheses in the main body of the text following a quotation or reference to their work.

Bibliography
List of works cited and used which appears at the end of the essay.

Brainstorming
Writing down all your ideas about a topic or question as they occur.

Case study
An in-depth investigation of a person, event or other phenomenon.

Commentary
A descriptive account of another text or work.

Conclusion
The major implications of a discussion or investigation.

Context
The background in which something occurs or is produced.

Empirical data
Data based on scientific observation.

Endnote
Reference appearing at the end of a piece of writing.

Et al.
Abbreviation indicating subsequent authors.

Figure
A photograph, diagram or other image.

Footnote
A reference appearing at the bottom of the page.

Grade boundaries
The criteria required to achieve certain grades.

Hypothesis
An initial claim which still needs to be tested.

Ibid.
Abbreviation referring to a text which has been cited in the previous footnote or endnote.

Introduction
The opening of an essay: it explains the question and the approach that will be taken.

Jargon
Specialist, scientific or technical language.

Journal
A collection of academic articles published on a regular basis.

Learning outcomes
The skills and knowledge you are expected to acquire.

Line break
Space imposed between one line of text and the next. Often used to indicate a new paragraph.

Linear plan
A plan in which one point proceeds from another.

Methodology
The specific approach taken to investigate or examine something.

Mind-map
A plan which identifies all the links existing between different points and examples.

Narrative
The art or technique of guiding your reader, similar to narrating a story.

Online sources (e.g. Athens)
Databases and journals which can be accessed on the internet.

Op. cit.
A reference to a text which has already been referenced, but not in the immediately preceding footnote or endnote.

Pagination
Page numbering and layout.

Paraphrase
To put in your own words or sum up.

Peer-review
The process in which academics review the work of other academics to ensure that it is of a publishable standard.

Plagiarism
Passing off someone else's work or ideas as your own.

Point – Example – Explanation (P.E.E.)
A simple way of structuring your paragraphs.

Polemic
Making a case for one position or argument rather than offering both or multiple sides.

Primary material/sources
Authentic data such as scientific reports, diaries, speeches and works of art.

Proofreading
Carefully checking written work for mistakes.

Quotation
The inclusion and acknowledgement of a statement written by someone else in your work.

Referencing/citation software
Programs which enable you to set up a database of references which are then automatically linked to your essay or Word document.

Register
The tone or type of language used.

Rhetoric
Language that relies on its own forcefulness to convince.

Rhetorical question
A statement posed in the form of a question for stylistic effect.

Secondary material/sources
Material that interprets and/or analyses primary sources.

Signpost
An indication of a new stage or development in the argument.

Strawman
A deliberately weak argument set up in order to destroy it.

Structure
The organisation of your essay.

Style guide
A detailed guide to how references should appear in an essay. Style guides vary depending on academic discipline.

Summary
A brief recap of major points.

Syntax
The word order in a sentence.

Tripartite structure
The organisation of an essay or argument into three distinct parts: thesis – antithesis – synthesis.

Unpacking a question
Explaining each part of a question and considering the limitations of its phrasing.

Word count
The total number of words used in your essay (usually including footnotes or endnotes but excluding bibliography and appendices).

Word limit
The maximum number of words allowed for a particular essay.